PROJECT RESET

The guide to your authentic life transformation

Ryan D. Lang, MD, MPH

Copyright © 2020 Ryan D. Lang. All rights reserved.

No part of this book may be reproduced, stored in a retrieval system, or transmitted by any means, electronic, mechanical, photocopying, recording, or otherwise without the prior written permission of the author.

Interior Design: Dxeralam

Cover Design: Pixel Studio

Content Editor: Shekeitha Jeffries

Copy Editor/Proofreader: Eric Benevides

Published in the United States of America.

ISBN 978-1-7363512-0-8

ISBN 978-1-7363512-1-5 (eBook)

DEDICATION

This book is dedicated to my mentor and friend, Dr. Gregory W. "Doc" Branch, for believing in me, inspiring me, challenging me, and seeing my potential in theatre.

Table of Contents

CHAPTER 1: INTRODUCTION: GET CLEAR 1

CHAPTER 2: TAKE STOCK OF YOUR VALUES 11

CHAPTER 3: GET COMFORTABLE MAKING HARD CHOICES 27

CHAPTER 4: TRUST YOURSELF 38

CONCLUSION 51

ACKNOWLEDGMENTS 54

ABOUT THE AUTHOR 57

CHAPTER 1

INTRODUCTION: GET CLEAR

PROJECT RESET

I can't remember the exact day or the moment that I decided that a reset was needed, but I know that it was sometime during the fall of 2020.

The year had already been upended by the coronavirus pandemic, and many of the goals and plans that I had for myself needed to be reconsidered. I was in a new job, in a new city, and I was miles away from the people who I cared for the most. However, it was in the midst of this upheaval that I found the time to not only stop and reflect upon my goals, but also get clear about what I really wanted and determine whether or not I was really getting it.

Perhaps you're in a place in your life where you feel frustrated and want to make a major change. It could be a new career, passion project, relationship development, or some other major undertaking that you have deferred for way too long. I can tell you that I have been there! Thankfully, I have gained some tools that helped me take the steps needed to undergo a major reset, and I want to pass some of these tools along to you so you can be successful in your own life reset!

> *It's an interesting place to be in when you finally get what you have worked hard for and **not** be totally satisfied.*

I was in that place for sure. I had spent over a decade as a student, graduated from some of the most prestigious universities, became a full-fledged board-certified physician in both internal medicine and general preventive medicine/public health, met and/or worked with some of the most prominent clinicians in the world, and secured a cushy job making six figures. By the world's standards, I had made it!

I was proud of what I had accomplished; however, once I finally landed a job that provided the freedom and financial stability that I desired, I still felt as though something was missing. I was getting ready to embark upon a new journey in my life. What I did not yet realize — but would soon! — was that this was a major sign that a life reset was on the horizon.

What is a life reset, exactly?

I define a life reset as *an intentional action toward a new way of being, thinking, and operating in any part of one's life.*

A life reset can be approached in many different areas of one's life, including identity, relationships (platonic, familial, and/or romantic), career, health, community involvement, and more. You might even consider how a life reset can be made in several areas at the same time! All things considered, the main purpose of a life reset is to craft a more authentic version of yourself.

It is important to emphasize that a reset is **intentional**. I strongly believe that the most effective choices in life are guided by clear intentions. When I read the book "The Seat of the Soul" by Gary Zukav, I got really clear on the importance of intention.

You can make a life reset for any number of reasons (or intentions). Maybe you want to make more money as a result of a life reset. Maybe you hope to find a committed relationship or a new community of support as the result of a life reset. Perhaps you simply want to live in alignment with your life purpose. All these and more are intentions that drive one toward making a life reset. As you continue to read, you'll also note that sometimes a life reset may arise from major life events in other areas that prompt one to consider pursuing a life reset.

During the time in which I was deciding the future of my career in medicine, I was also becoming more confident in my identity as a queer, non-binary person. The truth of my sexual and gender identities changed some of my closest relationships, including the relationship with my parents. After I shared my sexual orientation with my parents and began to clearly articulate how important my sexual orientation was to my identity, I slowly distanced myself from them once it became clear that I was not accepted for who I truly am. Eventually, I chose to end these relationships with my family and any other individuals who did not fully affirm and celebrate me in the fullness of my identity.

PROJECT RESET

As you might imagine, choosing to end relationships with my family and select others was extremely difficult, but I'm grateful for the support of close friends (and an excellent therapist). My inner circle helped me to process the grief of this loss, and now I am in a much better space, mentally and emotionally. While you might not have the same story I have, you might also consider the impact of other types of major life transitions (the loss of another relationship, death of a friend/loved one, getting married, having a child, losing a job, etc.) as it relates to initiating a reset in your own life. Pay close attention when you experience a major life transition, because it could have significant meaning for your life outside that one event.

Major life transitions can be blessings in disguise.

Though they can often be very stressful and bring pain at times, they are also big opportunities for change. Sometimes, major life transitions, planned or unplanned, can be the push needed to really shift into gear for a reset.

This was certainly the case for me, as I experienced a shift in my family connections.

But you don't necessarily have to go through a major life event in order to initiate a life reset. You might simply feel unchallenged or not respected in your current situation. Or, you might just feel as though you have experienced enough pain, frustration, or a sense of malaise in your current situation. These are also clear and justifiable reasons to plan for a reset.

In this process, it's important to cultivate the skills of self-reflection and self-awareness.

Often, if you take time to sit down in silence and think about your life, you will notice important information that comes to mind. I encourage you to take time to write these thoughts down without judgment. Also, consider the impact of any major life transitions and the thoughts that you have in regards to the events that are happening in your life. This is the beginning of your process toward a potential reset. There may be things that you really love about your life, and there may be some areas in your life that you want to improve. You may experience some events that magnify or intensify emotions that may have been hidden under the surface.

Write down your thoughts about these experiences, and be sure to include how they have impacted your life.

As you identify the areas of your life that are working and the areas that are not working, you will become clear about where you want to focus your efforts as you plan your life reset. Believe it or not, just admitting where a reset is needed or desired is a huge first step toward making a reset actually happen in your life!

You've now learned what a life reset is, and when you might consider implementing one in your own life. Keep reading as I share with you the framework I developed on how to execute a life reset. Consider this an iterative process, which means that you may have to go back to an earlier step multiple times in order to fully embrace the task of your life reset. I'm excited for you, and I believe in you.

GETTING STARTED!

1. Make sure you have a pen and a paper to write on as you read this book.

2. Begin by writing down the top three things that you really like about your life right now. If you can't think of three things right now, that's okay. Write down whatever you can think of at the moment.

3. Then, write down the top three things that you would change in your life right now. Try not to judge those thoughts, but simply see it as an exercise to identify what can be improved.

4. Hold onto these lists, as they will be very important as you go through the rest of this book.

PROJECT RESET

CHAPTER 2

TAKE STOCK OF YOUR VALUES

PROJECT RESET

After completing a second residency, I was asked to join the faculty of my program as Chief Resident for a year, after which I stayed on as a faculty member for an additional year. This job was fulfilling, as it allowed me to advise trainees while planning and executing programs and courses — things I did enjoy doing; however, I felt unchallenged because some of the main things that I really enjoyed doing were not part of my job and because there was a lack of variety. My contributions were appreciated; I really loved my co-workers, and I loved my institution. However, shortly into my second year on faculty, I just knew I was ready for something different.

By this point though, I had already done some major self-assessment about what it was that I liked and what I did not like about my job and my life in general (see the previous chapter for more on self-reflection).

I was clear that I desired a career that allowed independence and time for freedom. I wanted a career in which I could be a guide in self-reflection for others and in which I could serve others. I was very comfortable working by myself and actually enjoyed this! Though I do work well in teams and with others in general, I wanted time and space for myself in order to really thrive in the workplace. I discovered that working from home is much more desirable for me, as it provides the flexibility I need to have more ownership over my schedule.

I took time to identify my values.

Your values are so important, as they are the compass that helps to direct you toward what is right for you. While your values are typically influenced by who raised you and what their values are, you have the freedom and the right to determine your own values for yourself. That means that your values may change, as you learn more about what you actually want.

In my role as an internal medicine doctor, evaluating and treating patients in the outpatient clinic and in the hospital, I learned how important the values of hard work (often prioritized over personal time), compassion, and perseverance are in this career. While these are noble values and they are generally rewarded with a high salary, I did not wish to work long hours, nor did I want the responsibility of constantly being accountable to patients in this high-stress environment.

Even though I did my job well and was held in high regard by many patients, I did not hold myself with the same high regard. In not aligning my work with my values, I was not honoring myself. Therefore, I suffered.

It actually took many years for me to admit to myself that I was not in a career that aligned with my values. However, I soon found an opportunity to pivot towards a different career in preventive medicine that was in alignment with my values. I felt more at home in this specialty, even though I was beginning to see more clearly what I truly wanted.

Even while transitioning to preventive medicine, I continued to work as a part-time internal medicine physician, evaluating and treating hospitalized patients during shifts once or twice a month for a few years, mostly to make some extra money and justify my years of internal medicine training. Soon enough, I knew what I needed to do. I admitted to myself that patient care was not my passion, and a few months later, I resigned my position.

As I made this choice, I began to feel more empowered. I felt encouraged that I could actually make decisions that moved me not only in the direction of what mattered most to me, but also away from what did not feel right.

I reflected upon the values that kept me committed to a career path that I did not love. The value of persistence definitely served me well in completing my clinical training, but no longer served me once I discovered that I needed a change. The values of respect and external validation kept me tied to a career that brought me recognition for my accomplishments, even though I did not like what I was doing.

I had to learn how to re-prioritize my values to ensure they aligned with my goals.

That meant that I needed to prioritize the value of my peace, even if it meant that I would make less money in a new career path. I also needed to prioritize my personal time because, without it, I would not have the energy or the desire to serve others. I also needed to prioritize my value of artistic expression, which I had buried deep down and was badly in need of nurturing.

For many years, I had performed as a vocalist in choirs and occasionally as a soloist for church functions. I knew that I had a strong talent in music and had briefly considered studying music when I was a senior in high school. And as a child, I had tried my hand at acting in a few school plays and a larger stage play. I had fallen in love with theatre ever since I attended my first Broadway musical in the summer of 2006. I had also strongly considered working in television and had a few brief stints interning with a nationally-syndicated talk show in medical school and later for a major TV news organization during my residency.

I found it hard to reconcile my interest in all these areas, and I began to believe that these experiences might simply be footnotes to my actual calling as a physician.

But, as a wise person once said, "Don't give up your daydream."

Soon, I found an opportunity to audition for a stage play/musical at my institution that would be directed by a mentor who also happened to be a Black physician trained at the same hospital.

While I was familiar with the group's production history, I felt intimidated by the audition process. I had completed an actor's audition workshop a year earlier, and it humbled me greatly! I knew that I was a novice, and I was afraid to embark upon a new venture in which I had little experience or guarantee of success.

I quickly had to learn that some of the greatest breakthroughs in life happen when we have the courage to step outside our comfort zones. This was definitely a major out-of-comfort-zone moment to audition for the production!

It was a small production by a local playwright, and casting for the production was taking place at my work institution! I cropped a photo from a recent photo shoot that I had done for a magazine interview for my institution and used it as my first actor headshot. I then prepared a few musical numbers for the audition, knowing that it was a gospel-oriented stage play.

I was nervous, but did my best to put on a spectacular audition for the stage director and the playwright who were both there. Days later, I was cast in a supporting role in the play!

As I prepared for the role and found myself on stage, I found out how much I absolutely loved the experience. The play went very well, and that experience gave me the confidence I needed to audition for another musical with the same company/director months later. The second time around, I was cast in a lead role! It was a more thrilling experience, and I didn't quite know it at the time, but I was bitten by the acting bug.

Shortly thereafter, I had auditioned for and was later offered a supporting role in a third stage play/musical!

As I became more invested in acting, I began to see the endless possibilities available to me and I was excited! My value of artistic expression became more apparent through fashion and an interest in other forms of art as well, but I was unsure exactly how this would fit in with my already established career in medicine.

It's okay to not have all the answers at first. As you continue to grow, you'll discover more about yourself and what your values are.

PROJECT RESET

The key to increased self-awareness is listening to yourself and reflecting on what brings you joy. You must then identify opportunities to pursue those things, even if it's on a very small scale. For me, that meant finding community theatre roles for which to audition and even just attending shows whenever possible so that I can study other actors and learn the craft through observation.

As you find these opportunities, you will meet others who have the same interests, and you will begin to build a network of individuals who can provide useful guidance toward what you love. While in some cases, this might remain a hobby, you may be surprised at how small connections and opportunities may grow into larger ones as you remain invested.

I was pleasantly surprised by the opportunities that came for me to stay involved in acting, even with my "day job." However, these opportunities inspired me more to find more acting roles and learn more about the art of acting. As I got more experience in auditioning and landing roles, my confidence level in my skill and ability to find work increased. Also, I felt more motivated to keep going, and my values of creativity and artistic expression were solidified more.

As you take stock of your values and prioritize them, you may also have some discoveries about what works for you and what does not. As your values awareness increases, try to find new experiences and opportunities to "test out" whether certain activities align with your values. As you do this, it will become clearer for you what you value the most, and you can effectively honor yourself in pursuing that which brings you the most joy.

Your values are unique to you and may be very different from what another individual values. Therefore, it is important to go about the process of identifying your personal values without comparison or the pressure of making sure that your values are acceptable to others. It may require you to do things very differently than others and possibly identify a mismatch (or several) in values that you hold and the values of those around you. If this happens, do not panic. Get clear on what brings you joy and hold firm to that under all circumstances. You'll be grateful that you did!

TAKE ACTION!

1. If you don't do this already, make a calendar of every activity you have for the upcoming week.

2. Also, if you don't already, take note of whatever items you have spent using any discretionary income from the past week.

3. After making this calendar, take note of what types of activity you spend the most time doing. Also, take note of the types of things on which you spend the most of your discretionary income.

4. Write down what you consider to be the core reasons why you have decided to invest your time and money into these activities and things. There's no limit to this activity. Write whatever comes to mind.

5. After writing, try to see if you can consolidate your thoughts into themes. For example, say that you wrote "I spend $50 on eating at

restaurants this week because I enjoy trying new restaurants with friends in new areas of my city" and "I spent three hours this week going to social/networking events for Black mothers," you might consider themes such as "trying new things" or "socializing with others."

6. Make a new list with all your themes, and you can name this your "values" list.

7. Once you have written out these values, try to order them by priority for you ("1" is highest priority). Try not to consider what other people would choose or what you "should" choose as your priorities, but simply try to list your values according to what feels right for you.

8. After you have prioritized your values, consider what areas of your life seem to align with this list and areas where there may be misalignment. Think about what may be contributing to this. Also, consider that it is common to have values that might conflict

with each other, making it difficult to justify certain decisions or commitments. In this case, reassess which value is more important to you and consider why that is the case.

9. Consider putting this list of values up in an area where you can see it prominently and refer to it regularly. This can remind you of what your values are as you move forward in completing the following steps.

CHAPTER 3

GET COMFORTABLE MAKING HARD CHOICES

I eventually reached the point where change was necessary.

Change is not often easy to handle. We are wired as human beings to gravitate toward situations and people who make us feel safe. It's a protective mechanism that can serve us well in many cases. However, change can often cause us to feel as though we are unsafe because it can force us to reach outside what is familiar.

While I was excited to do something new, I still felt uneasy about leaving the city where I was. I had invested so much time in building connections and friendships in that city over the last seven years, and the prospect of losing many of those connections and starting all over felt daunting. I knew how much effort and time it took to feel comfortable there, and I did not want to go through the trouble of going back to square one in a new city and state where I had no strong connections.

I was worried about other things, such as the cost of living, brutal winters, how I would meet new friends, and more. Still, I knew that this was a change that I needed to make for personal growth.

> *What helped me make it through the initial apprehension was the reminder that I could always make a **new** choice if the original choice no longer served me.*

So many times, people become paralyzed by the process of making hard choices. They fear what will happen if they make the "wrong" choice, and I used to have this same problem. I would rack my brain for long periods of time in order to consider every factor I could in order to maximize my chances of making the best choice. You may have said that I was indecisive, but I considered myself to be *extremely* deliberate.

And because I am and always have been impeccable with my word, I believed that making a choice for myself was making a commitment to myself and that I could not break that commitment under any circumstances.

And with this reasoning, if I made a choice that did not work out in the way in which I wanted it to, I would often feel dejected and possibly hopeless, feeling that I was committed to that choice for the long haul with no opportunity for recourse.

My fear of making major decisions became almost non-existent once I reminded myself that I am in the driver's seat of my life and that I can always make a new choice!

This was absolutely life-changing for me. I felt like I was so powerful with this new self-awareness, and I felt free to really live life on my own terms. I was done feeling irrationally tied down to people or things that no longer served me.

With this assurance, I pressed forward in applying for a new job. I participated in a remote interview with members of the team, and after a few minutes of debriefing by the team privately, I was offered the job on the spot! I was ecstatic and could not wait to jumpstart my next chapter. I felt confident that if my choice worked out differently from what I expected, I had the freedom to change my mind.

You may face some tough challenges and decisions as you embark on your life reset. As you go through the process of making hard choices, it's important to do some key things:

1. **Consider your values and how those values are prioritized.** If you have not already done this, I encourage you to go back to Chapter 2 and go through the "Take Action!" steps at the end of the chapter. As you look over your values, it will become clearer to you what choices align with your primary values and which choices may potentially go against your values. Definitely take note of this as you move

forward, and do not overlook this very important step!

2. **Weigh the pros and cons of your various options.** In making a pros and cons list for each option, you may think about new aspects of the various options that you might not have considered previously. As you do this exercise, you will also be reminded of what is important to you and what your values are. As a bonus step, you might also write next to each pro or con what value you have considered as you have written it down.

3. **Talk to other people, specifically people who may have gone through the same decision-making process before you.** In asking them targeted questions about how they arrived at the decision, you may receive valuable information that will further illuminate what choice feels right for you. You might also learn information about a potential option that you

may not have previously considered, and that might provide clear guidance for you in choosing one option over another!

PROJECT RESET

Even after doing this work, you still might feel some trepidation as you make major decisions and changes in your life. It's important to realize that this feeling is normal, and it's okay to feel this way. But then, after you have allowed yourself the space to feel that apprehension, move forward boldly toward what you want. **There will likely be unanswered questions that remain.** There will be people who would advise you to do things differently from what you may feel is right for you. There may be concerns that might tempt you to fall back and do nothing. In spite of all these concerns, I encourage you to make the choice that scares you the most, but that you know is right for you.

And if it makes you feel any better, I'll reiterate that you can always find an opportunity to do things differently. You do have the option to make a different choice if the one that you've made does not work out the way you would have liked, even if it requires a little bit of additional time and sacrifice.

TAKE ACTION!

1. Think about a difficult decision that you had to make recently. What made it difficult for you to make that decision? Write down your answer to this.

2. What steps do you go through as you make a major decision? Write these steps down. Have these steps worked for you in the past? What do you think would make the process of deciding less cumbersome for you? Write down any thoughts you might have regarding new strategies for decision making and consider tools provided earlier in the chapter.

3. What are your non-negotiables? What is it that you are unwilling to compromise on regarding your values? Make sure that is clear as you move forward in making a decision.

4. Try to think about the possible outcomes with any option. In other words, how would your

life look with each potential option? Write down a sample of your life in each circumstance, and take note of what option seems most or least acceptable for you. This will also be helpful for you as you consider a path forward.

CHAPTER 4

TRUST YOURSELF

When hard choices and situations no longer make you freeze in fear, it becomes easier to listen to your internal compass in guiding you forward.

Months after my last interview, I moved to another new state to begin my new job. By the time I began my new job, the coronavirus pandemic had been going on for months, forcing most businesses that could to shift their work to remote operations given the risk of viral transmission. Once I was settled, I arranged to work from home like the rest of my co-workers. I was extremely grateful to have a job, even as the economy worsened and millions of Americans had become unemployed.

As I acclimated to the new job, it was only a few weeks before I knew the truth. The job paid very well and definitely supported the lifestyle that I desired. I could not have asked for better co-workers.

Still, once again, I knew that I was not pursuing my true calling.

For me, that awareness began with the simple understanding that I once again did not feel challenged. I was definitely learning new information and gaining skills in an area that I had not worked before. However, I knew that many of the strengths and abilities that I had developed over the years prior were not being used.

Initially, I was satisfied to just coast through the job and not complain about what I was experiencing. I had to really dig deep and reflect on what I wanted my work life to look like. I needed to get clear on what I already knew about my current situation.

When you embark on pursuing your life purpose, you must get to the point where you trust yourself.

Trusting yourself is a very important skill that requires lots of practice. We all have regular opportunities to check in with ourselves on what we have chosen and whether it feels right for us. You also have regular opportunities to check in with yourself *before* making choices to determine whether it feels right.

> *One thing I know about trusting yourself is that the better you are at identifying how your body and soul speak to you, the easier it then becomes to practice trusting yourself regularly.*

My body speaks very clearly through my chest and my gut. If I'm considering something that does not feel right in my spirit, I will likely experience a gnawing pain or discomfort in one or both of those areas. Most times, these are very subtle, but at other times, they can be more pronounced. Typically, those sensations alone are sufficient for me to pay attention and make changes where needed or go in a different direction altogether.

In the past, when I ignored those initial signs, I might sweat or experience trouble sleeping. These are my body's warning signs that I am potentially about to dishonor myself by choosing something that is not for me.

Now, while I do believe that intuition can speak to us through our bodies, as mine does for me, it would be irresponsible of me to say that bodily signs and symptoms solely represent signals of intuition. You should also make sure that if some of these signs are frequent and/or severe, you seek medical attention. I get checkups regularly to make sure that I am healthy, and I have learned through an understanding of my body to more accurately determine what next steps should be taken for myself.

Some individuals may experience signs differently, such as through life experiences in other ways, a sense of mental fog or restlessness, or perhaps even through dreams, which represent the subconscious mind. There are many other ways in which you might receive messages that guide you internally. I encourage you to determine what they are and then write down how you experience messages to yourself from yourself. That way, you can become clear on what to look for or listen for as you practice trusting yourself.

As I took time to listen to myself about what I felt, it became clear that another change was needed. Furthermore, I was clear that my true life purpose was to inspire and empower others through my authenticity and creativity to live in their truth. In doing this, I reassessed my life experiences and values to determine what the next best step would be for me. The resounding answer that my soul gave to me was to pursue a career as a professional actor.

As you begin to trust yourself, you will likely face doubts. You'll probably have some self-doubt, especially if the direction you're facing is different from where you have gone before. The more comfortable you are in your current space, the more challenging it may be for you to accept what you feel, especially if it's prompting a major change. I can tell you for sure that I know how this feels from personal experience!

You might even face doubt from others. If you are used to going along with what other people think or say without checking in with yourself, then there may be some resistance from those who are used to seeing you do what makes them feel secure.

I encourage you to detach yourself from the responses of other people as you do what feels right to you.

RYAN D. LANG, MD, MPH

PROJECT RESET

I wouldn't want for you to second-guess yourself because someone else might have an unfavorable opinion or take on what you have already determined is for you. Try being selective about who has access to you or who receives information about what you're up to in order to avoid messing up the skill you're building in trusting yourself. Soon enough, you'll reach the point where your confidence in yourself and the trust that you have in yourself is relatively unshakable.

Once again, I considered what made me excited and what activities really enhanced my life and found myself thinking about acting. Getting into character and being able to entertain using my craft was what I thought about almost every day. The more I sat with that feeling, the more it prompted me to take action toward doing what needed to be done to continue pursuing acting as a career.

While I had been cast in another production earlier in the year, that gig had been canceled due to the public health emergency. But because I trusted myself and knew clearly what I really wanted, I did not let the effects of the pandemic deter me from holding on to my clarity. I found out about a new production for which I could audition virtually. I submitted an audition package and was offered a supporting role in the production! I trust that this is the beginning of many more acting roles to come.

The immense gratification I received being on stage was one that I could not deny had a major impact on me. I knew I was in my element as an actor and that my primary value of creative expression would be satisfied. Even though there would be a lot of hard work and sacrifice ahead of me, I was energized by the prospect of doing what brought me true joy.

One thing I believe is that when you are committed to a goal and trust that you are capable of achieving that goal, you will do what is necessary to bring that vision to fruition. I had and continue to have a confidence so great in my acting skill and ability that nothing will stop me from working toward becoming a professional actor because that is what I believe is for me. That doesn't mean that the journey will be easy or that success will happen overnight. However, I have the dedication and passion required to do what needs to be done in order to pursue this career path, and I trust myself that I can and do make decisions that are in my best interest.

I believe that you are just as powerful and have the same ability to trust yourself to do what is in your best interest as well. As you cultivate this skill and learn to become confident in your inner voice, the opportunities to align yourself with your true calling become even clearer to identify and pursue.

TAKE ACTION!

1. What parts of your life do you feel go against what you really want? What impact does this have on your life?

2. What signals, if any, do you recall having received before committing to a path that did not feel right for you? Do you feel anything as you consider this topic now? If so, write down what you feel. If it's a bodily signal, write down where you feel it.

3. What people, places, and/or things could possibly impact your ability to remain true to yourself? What is it about those people, places, and/or things that contributes to this?

4. Looking at your answer to question 1, how would your life change if you were able to shift toward going after what you really want in the areas you identified?

5. What might stop you from putting this process into action? How can you plan ahead to address this or prevent any barriers to you being able to go for what you really want?

CONCLUSION

Making a life reset is hard, yet possible. You may feel as though there's too much going on right now for you to initiate a reset or that you're not ready yet. I encourage you to consider using the framework I developed, and then take action!

Your life reset might not involve making a major career transition; however, the strategies that I've provided are key to any form of life reset that you may be considering. The year 2020 brought extreme challenges. However, in the pain of those experiences, many people began to truly take stock of their lives and what was or was not working. For some, this new awareness allowed challenges in their lives that were small and perhaps commonly avoided previously to be magnified. However, in bringing these issues to the surface during the course of a tumultuous year, a new opportunity was granted to be proactive in making changes where necessary.

Now that you have the tools to take action, don't delay. Because you have this book, it's very likely that you are in the mindset for your life reset to happen now. Don't miss the opportunity to capitalize on this motivation. Start today!

Establish a timeline to help you as you work toward fully executing your life reset. Be realistic and allow yourself enough time to fully devote toward this undertaking. I recommend selecting an entire year, because it's just long enough to make progress, yet short enough to keep you engaged and on track and not to become complacent. It's totally doable!

You may consider working with a coach to help keep you accountable as you Reset Your Life. If you feel that this is something that would help you, then visit my website at www.drryanlang.com, follow me on Instagram (@blackmillennialcoach), or "like" me on Facebook (Ryan - Black Millennial Coach) to see how I might be able to work with you as your personal coach in achieving your own authentic transformation. I believe in you, and I want to see you succeed as you work toward your life reset!

ACKNOWLEDGMENTS

Writing this book was such a blessing for me, and I could not end it without saying thank you to the people who helped me in completing it.

To Shekeitha Jeffries, my book content editor, personal coach, former work colleague, and close friend – Thank you so much!!! When I asked if you could review my book, you didn't hesitate to say yes. You went above and beyond in providing honest and comprehensive feedback. I am so grateful for you and your support with this project and so many of my personal and professional aspirations! And thank you for the encouragement when I needed a boost to keep me focused on the prize!

To Eric Benevides, my copy editor and proofreader – Thank you for being thorough and for your positive words to encourage me as I prepared this book.

To Sharon Michaels – Thank you for being there and for providing a simple "How can I support you?" when I shared that I was writing this book, as well as following through regularly to share resources whenever you could.

To Tristan Desinor – Thank you for providing support and guidance for not only this project, but also for my social media platforms and business.

To Harvey Kennedy-Pitt, Jessica Murphy, and Shayla Pedersen-Guy – Thank you so much for your support and encouragement along the way and a message to keep going even when things got tough!

To Black Beetle Health, LLC – Thank you for having me as a panelist and collaborator for your events and for valuing my input and expertise while helping to expand my reach as a coach.

To Shereka Dunston – Thank you for being a great role model and a supporter/cheerleader in my growth as a coach.

PROJECT RESET

To everyone who purchased this book – Thank you for your support and for believing in me as I believe in you!

ABOUT THE AUTHOR

Ryan D. Lang, MD, MPH (he/they) is a certified life coach focused on empowering Black millennials to find their life purpose and navigate major life transitions. He is also an actor and a dually board-certified internal medicine and preventive medicine physician. Dr. Lang previously served as a medical unit intern with both *The Dr. Oz Show* and ABC News. He is a graduate of Oakwood University, Vanderbilt University School of Medicine, and the Johns Hopkins Bloomberg School of Public Health. He received his life coach certification from the Life Coach Training Institute in 2020. He was born and raised in Huntsville, Alabama.

www.drryanlang.com

Instagram: @blackmillennialcoach

Facebook: http://www.facebook.com/blackmillennialcoach

www.ingramcontent.com/pod-product-compliance
Lightning Source LLC
Chambersburg PA
CBHW020915080526
44589CB00011B/605